OFFICES
for Small Spaces

OFFICES
for Small Spaces

Alejandro Bahamón

HDi

HARPER
DESIGN
international

An Imprint of HarperCollins*Publishers*

Publisher: **Paco Asensio**

Editor and Text: **Alejandro Bahamón**

Editor in Chief: **Haike Falkenberg**

Research: **Cristina Montes**

Art Director: **Mireia Casanovas Soley**

Graphic Design: **Agustí Argüelles and Ana Gutiérrez**

Layout: **Ignasi Gracia Blanco**

First published in 2004 by:
Harper Design International, an imprint of HarperCollins Publishers
10 East 53rd Street
New York, NY 10022

Distributed throughout the world by:
HarperCollins International
10 East 53rd Street
New York, NY 10022
Tel.: (212) 207-7000
Fax: (212) 207-7654

HarperCollins books may be purchased for educational, business, or sales
promotional use. For information, please write:
Special Markets Department
HarperCollins Publishers Inc.
10 East 53rd Street
New York, NY 10022

Library of Congress Cataloging-in-Publication Data

Bahamón, Alejandro.
  Offices for small spaces / Alejandro Bahamón.
     p. cm.
  ISBN 0-06-059845-X (hardcover)
  1. Office decoration. 2. Small rooms. 3. Interior architecture. I. Title.
  NK2195.O4B34 2004
  725'.23–dc22

                    2004001051

Editorial project

LOFT Publications
Via Laietana, 32 4º Of. 92
08003 Barcelona. Spain
Tel.: +34 932 688 088
Fax: +34 932 687 073
e-mail: loft@loftpublications.com
www.loftpublications.com

Printed by:
Tesys, Indústries gràfiques. Sabadell, Spain

DL: B-6.498-2004

First printing, 2004

SUMMARY

Introduction

This book addresses two important architectural and interior design elements that inform the creation of modern offices. The first factor is the notion of highly aesthetic space—a break with formal convention—where technological advances are key to bringing about functional solutions. Firms emphasize their corporate images to communicate their unique identities. Different strategies are used in each office space to impart that identity so that the design projects become laboratories of ideas for architects and designers. The second factor is the incessant demand for workspace, especially in the big cities, which increases speculation and forces companies to make do with the small amount of space available. To facilitate the efficient reduction of office space technological advances, new communications networks and certain atypical work arrangements are used. The unique characteristics of contemporary design and the lack of space have led to the birth of a phenomenon of great interest to both designers and any company that must adapt itself to a reduced workspace: the small office.

The design strategies for each small office are as varied as the existing circumstances of each space. We can, however, point out a few features that the need to scale down has made common to all projects. The first section of this volume looks at common furniture elements and identifies certain issues that need to be addressed when planning this type of project. The second section examines various design projects for small offices, demonstrating a variety of issues and possible solutions. The small space available forces the companies and designers to prioritize the functions of a space when designing the offices. In some cases, conference rooms take up most of the space because they are the company's most frequently used area. In other cases all the work furniture can be easily stored away so the office space can be put to other uses when necessary. In still others the carefully chosen chairs become pivotal to the flexible use of the space. The 25 projects included in this book—involving small offices from around the world—bear witness to a great diversity of situations that must be resolved with ingenuity and creativity.

FURNITURE

Partitions

Internal partitions are highly important in any office project. New materials and light structures have made the inflexibility of cubicle dividers a thing of the past. A project for a small space should simplify these divisions as much as possible, ensuring that they take up the minimum amount of space and provide the privacy required in each case. Traditional materials such as glass and wood are now complemented by others, such as polycarbonate, fiberglass, and metallic mesh.

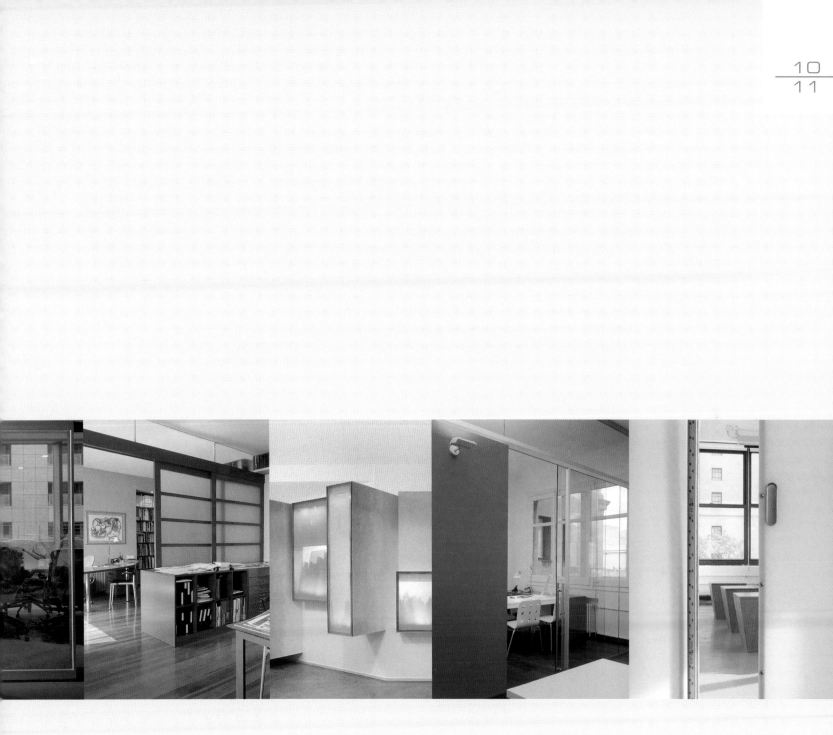

Conference rooms

Conference rooms are the most important spaces in a company for many office design projects—not just because of the face the company wants to present to the public, but also because of its internal work dynamic. These spaces are fundamental to expressing the corporate image and work philosophy. In some cases they may be very formal, while in others they may be run-of-the-mill, cluttered with the paraphernalia of the work routine.

Chairs

In addition to their ergonomic qualities, fundamental to the comfort of those who spend so many hours seated, chairs play an important role in expressing the image and supporting the operation of many offices. Chairs can define the company's character while also providing flexible seating and easily removeable options within the space.

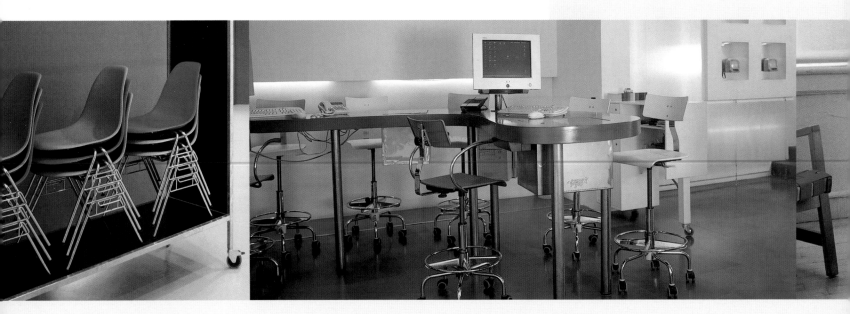

Shelving

The storage of work materials, books, or documents is fundamental to an office design project. Often, shelving is used as a basic design element in order to project a certain image. Because of their prominence, shelves play an important role in interior design. They can function as internal dividers, line the walls, or act as movable modules.

Work surfaces

Desks, tables, and counters are perhaps the only unavoidable elements in any workspace. Their shape, size, and placement are determined entirely by the type of work to be performed. Tall work surfaces are better for tasks that can be completed relatively quickly or for customer service. Other work surfaces function as conference tables or can be moved about so they can be combined or stored.

PROJECTS

ARCHITECT: GLEN IRANI ARCHITECTS
PHOTOGRAPHY: UNDINE PRÖHL
LOCATION: VENICE, CA, UNITED STATES
DATE OF CONSTRUCTION: 2002
AREA: 775 SQ. FT.

Glen Irani Architects

This design is the result of the architect's desire to combine his family home with his workplace. Since he spends most of his time in the office, he chose an exceptional location: the 775-square-foot office occupies the entire lower floor, is right next to the garden, and has direct access to the outdoor pool. The interior was carefully designed to accommodate a number of activities: recreational use of the garden, small social or professional receptions, after-hours reading, and weekend leisure activities.

To make the best use of the available space and maximize flexibility, the architect designed four wheeled workstations that could be easily moved along a rail for storage in the rear. The electrical equipment and the lighting fixtures, also designed to facilitate movement of the desks, are independent of them.

The narrow lot and the position of the pool necessitated a longitudinal plan for the office space.

The work modules consist of a curved piece of sheet metal that functions as a work surface and lateral support and connects to the long rail.

The designer made the best use of the long space by placing the workstations one behind the other, aligned with the swimming pool.

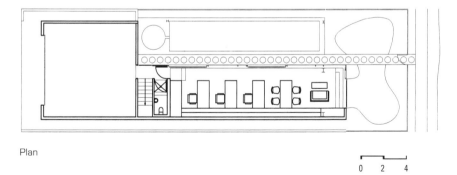

Plan

0 2 4

Placing the office at a level slightly below the swimming pool creates a dramatic effect and allows for a higher ceiling in the office.

The storage cabinets at the workstations and those
attached to the side wall are made of plywood
covered with highly resilient colored laminate.

A reading nook sits right next to the building's rear garden.

ARCHITECTS: FRANCISCO PARDO, JULIO AMEZCÚA
PHOTOGRAPHY: ADOLFO PARDO
LOCATION: MEXICO CITY, MEXICO
DATE OF CONSTRUCTION: 2003
AREA: 600 SQ. FT.

Office at 103

This temporary structure is part of the urban landscape of modern Mexico City. Small units such as this are erected on the roofs of buildings as a partial solution to the space limitations of this city of 25 million inhabitants. They function as utility rooms, restrooms, homes, guardhouses, storage space, and clothes-drying areas, among other purposes. This light structure was fitted out as a multidisciplinary office shared by several professionals in creative fields.

Back in 2001, the founding members joined forces to come up with a shared strategy for developing new design projects. The decision to share space and logistics was the result of their desire to pool their multi-disciplinary knowledge so each member could contribute his or her personal experience to the project. The structure itself is a metal-framed translucent 22- by 11.5-foot box, divided into 4- by 8-foot sections. Each module, and the entire grouping, is demarcated by panels made of different materials, arranged according to the use assigned to each.

To minimize its impact on the roof's surface, the metal framework rests slightly above it.

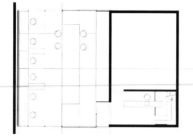

Plan

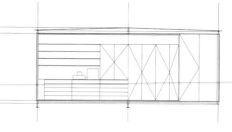

Interior elevation

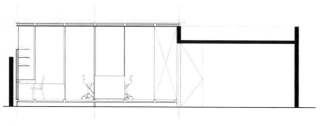

Interior elevation

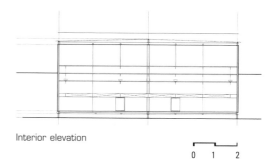

Interior elevation

0   1   2

The interior of the office is free of dividers, and the façades that are not adjacent to other structures are constructed of translucent polycarbonate panels.

ARCHITECT: LEROY STREET STUDIO ARCHITECTS
PHOTOGRAPHY: PAUL WARCHOL
LOCATION: NEW YORK, NY, UNITED STATES
DATE OF CONSTRUCTION: 1999
AREA: 850 SQ. FT.

Leroy Street Studio

Two young architects, colleagues since their days at Yale University, decided to restore a small, rundown store/warehouse in Manhattan's West Village and fit it out as their own architecture studio. The shared passion for innovation and construction technology that led them to work together in the first place was also the jumping-off point for the remodeling of this small building, typical of Greenwich Village commercial premises. Its basic structure, with the brick outer walls providing structural support and windows facing the street, made it relatively easy to use the space to good advantage.

The rehabilitation involved opening up the interior by demolishing some existing dividers that limited the amount of light received in the rear. These were replaced by thin sliding doors that emphasize the interrelatedness of the entire space, but ensure greater privacy in selected areas. To make the two-story unit feel more like a single space, a very light metal staircase that permits visual contact between the two levels was installed.

A metal grille covers both sides of the staircase, allowing natural light to shine through and creating an indoor courtyard effect right in the middle of the space.

The staircase dominates this office. Besides connecting the two levels, it adds great formal richness.

ARCHITECT: JOHN PAWSON ARCHITECTS
PHOTOGRAPHY: RICHARD GLOVER, DENNIS GILBERT/VIEW
LOCATION: LONDON, UNITED KINGDOM
DATE OF CONSTRUCTION: 2000
AREA: 800 SQ. FT.

Pawson Office

The offices of John Pawson Architects are an accurate reflection of this English architect's interior design and construction work over the course of his prolific career. They occupy the ground floor —which includes the entrance—and basement of a former industrial space in north London. Major goals for the project were to provide excellent natural lighting, retain the character of the original property, and provide for flexible use of the space.

Much of the renovation work involved removing clutter and installing state-of-the-art technology, while retaining the open plan and the industrial esthetic. From the entrance, which affords a panoramic view of the city, stairs of polished concrete lead down to the basement work area. A large, long work surface in the center of the space frees up the perimeter and emphasizes the clean lines.

From the ground floor entrance visitors can enjoy a panoramic view of this industrial area right behind St. Pancras Station.

The two white walls on either side of the stairs to the lower level create a dramatic, almost ceremonial effect.

Straight lines, pure shapes, and the color white
create a bright, peaceful atmosphere, subtly
accentuated by the lighting.

A large opening at the ground floor level allows
natural light to flood the office space below.

The large central desk has different levels to provide well-defined areas for work, equipment, and electrical fixtures.

The central desk allows for great flexibility without the need for complex solutions or shifting furniture around.

ARCHITECT: ARCHIKUBIK
PHOTOGRAPHY: MIQUEL TRES
LOCATION: BARCELONA, SPAIN
DATE OF CONSTRUCTION: 2001
AREA: 860 SQ. FT.

British Summer

British Summer, located in Barcelona, Spain, is a company that sells courses abroad for children and adults. Its location (at the end of a street and right off high-traffic areas) and the client's desire to create a strong public image were the points of departure for the design process. The office had to create a system and an aesthetic conducive to a dynamic relationship between the workers and the clientele.

Several design strategies work together to create an interesting play of situations from the entrance all the way back to the workstations. An interaction with an urban flavor is established by the polycarbonate lighting employed in the entrance area, and different atmospheres are created by changing the colors of the fluorescent lights farther back. In this way, the business's presence is signaled to passerby in a striking manner without falling back on external components such as banners. The play of geometric shapes, the large public service area, and the lack of clutter all help to effectively attract the public.

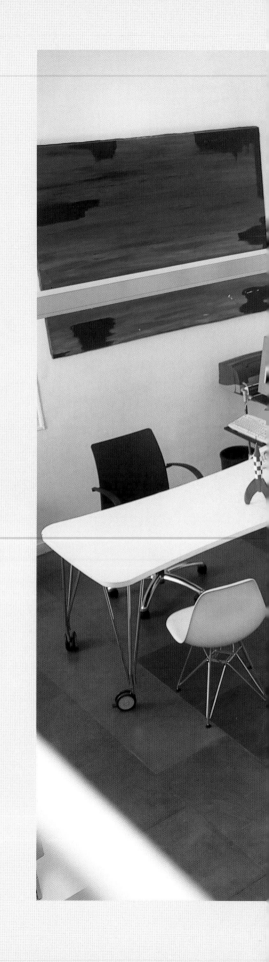

The play of colors changes with the time of day or season of the year: yellow for day, blue for night, red for summer, purple for winter, and so forth.

A somewhat more private small office, which also functions as a conference room, was installed in the upper part of the two-story space.

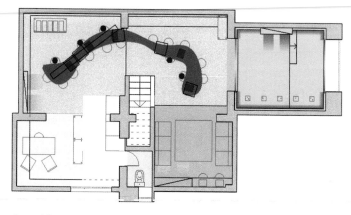

Ground floor

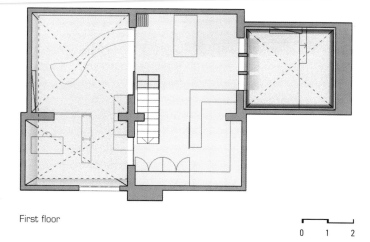

First floor

0   1   2

Part of the interior is dominated by a large table
where the staff can work and assist the public.

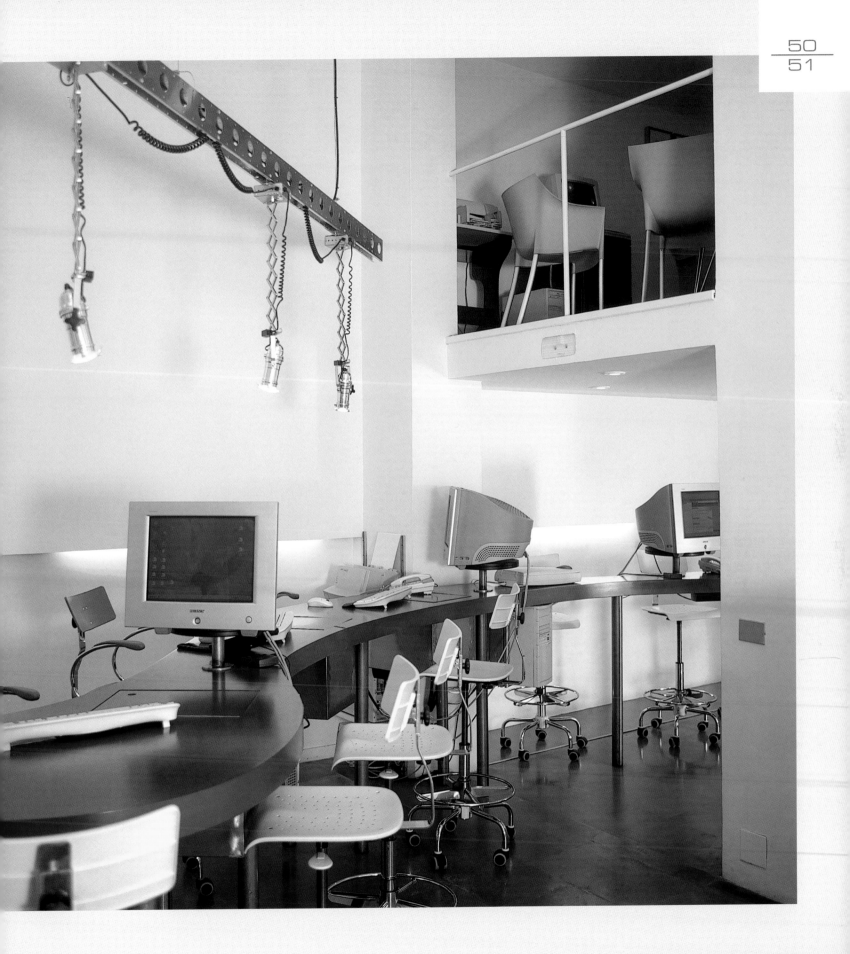

The high table, wheeled chairs, and furnishings that are suspended or flush with the walls allow for an uninterrupted view of the floor, enhancing the feeling of spaciousness.

ARCHITECTS: ROGER HIRSCH ARCHITECT, MYRIAM CORTI
PHOTOGRAPHY: MINH + WASS
LOCATION: NEW YORK, NY, UNITED STATES
DATE OF CONSTRUCTION: 2002
AREA: 624 SQ. FT.

Graphic Design Office

Given the tiny proportions of this space, less than 650 square feet, the major challenge for this project was to achieve a flexible arrangement that could be transformed to permit totally different uses. The idea was to be able to hide most of the elements that make up "office space" in order to provide a totally clear space that could be used for other purposes. The solution was to demolish the old partitions that divided the space to make room for a mechanism with which the clients themselves could literally transform the office.

This mechanism is a freestanding structure that closes to hide the office or opens to reveal it, integrating it with the space. Two shets of birch plywood sit in a metal guide and fold, thanks to a central hinge. Each panel, in turn, has two small swinging doors that provide access to office material when the system is closed. In accordance with the client's specific needs, the storage units were custom-built for the objects they contain.

The openings in the two panels are aligned when the panels are folded to create an interior window that provides light for the work area.

The panels are easy to move, thanks to the steel guide that supports the structure and the wheels.

ARCHITECT: SLADE ARCHITECTURE
PHOTOGRAPHY: JORDI MIRALLES
LOCATION: NEW YORK, NY, UNITED STATES
DATE OF CONSTRUCTION: 2000
AREA: 860 SQ. FT.

Bill Smith Studio

This former industrial property was transformed into offices for a graphic design agency specializing in children's books. The clients wanted the new space to be flexible enough to accommodate a staff that might increase in size during busy times, and they wanted it to have an urban theme incorporating the idea of favelas, typical Brazilian suburban shantytowns. In short, they wanted their new workplace to be totally informal and arranged so that each part of the whole could function autonomously.

The various workspaces are delimited by a system of shelves with metal posts commonly found in air-conditioning and mechanical systems. Additional pieces of mechanical equipment are used for more shelving and as work surfaces. Some of the room dividers are fiberglass, which is easy to set up and disassemble and allows light to pass through. The furnishings, mostly of recycled materials, are carefully placed to create a random effect while maximizing functionality.

The furnishings, custom designed for the project, are a constant reminder that children are the company's customers. They were also made to be easily moved within the space as needed.

The metal posts that support the shelving and allow for adjustment of shelf heights can be moved around and anchored anywhere, as needed.

Fiberglass panels make slim dividers that diffuse the natural light. The panels are anchored to the same types of structures as those used for the shelving.

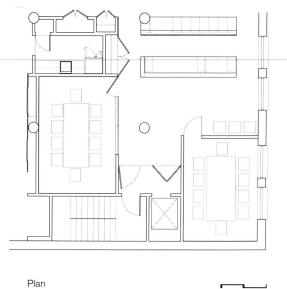

Plan

0   1   2

ARCHITECTS: ESCAPE*spHERE, MARTIN KUNATH
PHOTOGRAPHY: PEZ HEJDUK
LOCATION: VIENNA, AUSTRIA
DATE OF CONSTRUCTION: 2002
AREA: 860 SQ. FT.

ega

The design of the Vienna headquarters of ega—a new, semi-public cultural institution for women who are members of the Socialist Party of Austria—posed several challenges. First, there had to be a close relationship between the interior and the urban context, as if these offices were almost an extension of the public space of the street. In counterpoint to this notion was the idea of achieving a self-contained space with a peaceful atmosphere conducive to educational and cultural activities. And the new image had to be consistent with a commitment to the feminist movement: contemporary and open to all participants. Its close relationship to the urban environment was also based on the premise of attracting a varied audience.

The design creates a totally transparent space, open to the street, from which the classrooms at the rear can be seen. All existing interior partitions were removed and replaced with screens that are easy to move around. The textile material used for the screens makes both sides suitable for projecting images, and even makes it possible to use the reception area as additional classroom space.

The concrete benches are repeated outside the headquarters, reinforcing the close relationship with the interior.

A system of flexible screens and rails anchored to the original ceiling makes it simple to rearrange the interior divisions.

Simple shapes and flexible elements make it possible
to use the interior for many different activities.

In the main classroom, all partitions were eliminated
and a bar was installed for the participants' use.

From the outside, two large windows edged with
sheet metal frame the view of the interior and
define its relationship with the exterior.

The space was divided in a direction perpendicular to the office's only windows, taking the best advantage of the available natural light.

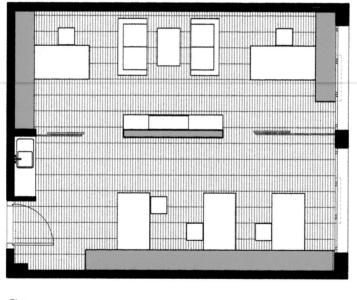

Plan

0   1   2

Orange is used as an accent color and is picked
up in some of the furnishings to highlight the
fixed components.

In the workers' area, desks can be added, removed, or combined in accordance with the agency's needs.

ARCHITECT: KLEIN DYTHAM ARCHITECTURE
PHOTOGRAPHY: KOZO TAKAYAMA
LOCATION: AKASAKA, TOKYO, JAPAN
DATE OF CONSTRUCTION: 1999
AREA: 860 SQ. FT.

BBH

The design for an advertising agency such as Bartle Bogle Hegarty demanded an imposing interior that would project the proper image in its new Tokyo office. BBH is growing and expects to need larger quarters in the near future. Thus, the project had to make the space over with components that could be easily dismantled when they need to be moved.

Located in a typical Tokyo office building, the space in question is rectangular, with windows at the back providing natural light. The walls and ceiling were not touched, since they will have to be turned over in their original condition when the space is vacated, so the design employed light components arranged to configure each work area.

The refurbishing brought out the best in the available space, using a linear plan to create a feeling of roominess. The U-shaped meeting room reflects concepts from traditional Japanese culture and seems to float above the bright red floor. Silver curtains afford privacy when necessary and darkness for viewing tapes or slides. Lacquered surfaces, the U shape that is repeated in the reception area furniture, and a combination of warm and fluorescent lighting have crafted a sparkling, luminous space.

The low, black-lacquered conference table and blue
cushions accentuate the project's references to
traditional Japanese culture.

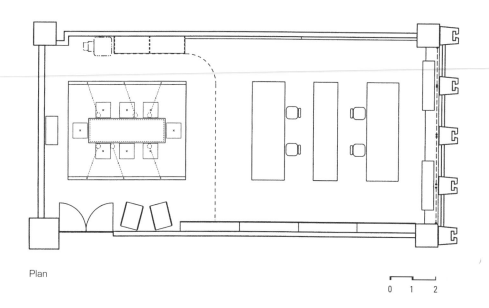

Plan

0 1 2

The furnishings—including, in this case, the meeting
room itself—project the image of a youthful,
innovative company.

ARCHITECT: OSKAR LEO KAUFMANN
PHOTOGRAPHY: IGNACIO MARTÍNEZ
LOCATION: MOBILE
DATE OF CONSTRUCTION: 2000
AREA: ADJUSTABLE

Fred

Fred is an expandable unit measuring 10 feet by 10 feet by 10 feet when closed, and up to 710 feet when fully extended on its rails. This is possible thanks to its design, with walls that slide in response to electronic controls. The interior is used as a workspace with restroom and kitchenette. Fred's versatility, lightness, and compactness—when closed—make it easy to transport and relocate. Once in position, the unit just needs to be hooked up to the utilities and electronically opened, and it's ready for use.

A strong, sturdy structure was needed to withstand a lot of movement, so high-quality, well-built, precision materials were used. The wooden framework used in the sections and the opening/closing system is completely covered by colored plywood panels, and the entrance boasts a large window. Furnishings and the other appurtenances needed for office operations are built into the unit, making Fred ideal for businesses on the go.

When the new location is chosen, the ground is leveled, the base is put in place, and the rails are positioned.

The inner box slides out over two rails on the bottom of the unit, doubling the amount of interior space.

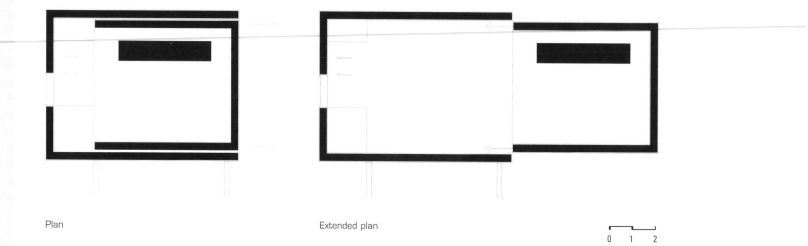

Plan   Extended plan

0   1   2

The interior is a totally open, flexible space with no dividers.

ARCHITECT: MESSANA O'RORKE ARCHITECTS
PHOTOGRAPHY: ELIZABETH FELICELLA
LOCATION: NEW YORK, NY, UNITED STATES
DATE OF CONSTRUCTION: 1998
AREA: 860 SQ. FT.

Messana O'Rorke Architects

When designing their own studio, architects Brian Messana and Toby O'Rorke saw an opening to project their image and their design ideals. This project clearly responds to both the conditions of the space and the company's functional and aesthetic needs. The space was bright and ample but narrow, and the challenge was to create a single, integrated setting that makes the most of its original character, but can be divided into different work areas.

The design concept was based on maximizing the sensation of spaciousness and natural lighting and creating a setting in which the space reveals itself gradually. This was achieved by dividing it into a series of sections that can be closed off in different ways, thus affording varying degrees of privacy and contact. The partitions, made of wooden frames and Plexiglas panels, brighten the rooms and make it possible to see what's going on in other parts of the office. The wooden cabinets are used for storage, as shelving, and as dividers to section off the conference room.

The components that divide the space, both the cabinets and the translucent panels, are floor-to-ceiling, emphasizing the division into independent areas.

The paneling material is transparent, and the openings create a unique and subtle relationship between the different rooms.

The internal layout is based on a longitudinal hall that connects the different rooms. The most public rooms are closest to the entrance, while the most private, such as the library/conference room, are at the rear of the studio.

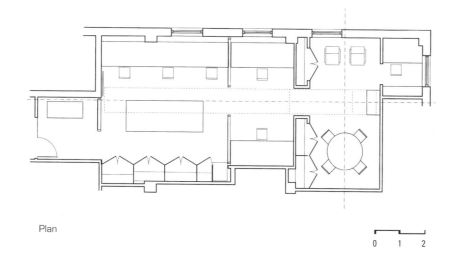

Plan

0   1   2

Placing the work tables up against the side walls frees the central area for workspace.

The translucent panels filter and distribute the
natural light that enters from above.

The room farthest from the entrance is the quietest
place in the office, a small library and
conference room.

ARCHITECT: JORDI HIDALGO
INTERIOR DESIGNER: DANIELA HARTMANN
PHOTOGRAPHY: EUGENI PONS
LOCATION: OLOT, SPAIN
DATE OF CONSTRUCTION: 2002
AREA: 860 SQ. FT.

Courtyard Office

This tiny office is the result of refurbishing a home's badly deteriorated rear courtyard—a chaotic space that had seen several haphazard changes over the years. This remodeling freed up the rear wall of the home and placed the new unit at the back of the parcel to create an open space, like a courtyard, between the new and old structures. Thus, the two activities were better separated, providing an exterior space that functions as a foyer and affording natural lighting for both units.

The refurbishment of this small, inaccessible space presented major challenges. For one thing, the opposite house limited the ability to maneuver materials and use a crane. Also, the builders had to preserve the lower level, which houses a small gym, and protect it from water. And. finally, the construction had to be completed in record time: two months. The solution was to set up a metal structure—preserving many of the original architectural elements—before demolishing the existing unit.

The glass façade integrates the interior of the office with the courtyard while making the most of the natural light.

The metal structure minimized the number of construction elements and resulted in a very light unit that communicates with the exterior.

In addition to unifying the area, the shiny floor creates a mirror effect, accentuating the feeling of spaciousness.

The movable furnishings and the elements that divide
the various rooms, but touch neither floor nor
ceiling, create a light, flexible image.

ARCHITECT: PROPELLER Z
PHOTOGRAPHY: PEZ HEJDUK
LOCATION: MOBILE
DATE OF CONSTRUCTION: 1999
AREA: ADJUSTABLE

Fast Forward

An office that contains a work of art could be the defining concept of this hybrid system, which offers the opportunity to sit down, recline, work at a computer, or store or display information. A horizontal platform from which parts are removed, the system forms a kind of sinuous labyrinth that can accommodate each artist's needs. Its shape and dimensions can be adapted to spaces of varying proportions and requirements.

The component itself dramatically transforms the space it occupies. This single piece is the solution to issues of function, image, and flexibility. Parts of the whole can become independent modules, usable elsewhere as reception desks or conference tables, creating a universal image that adapts to any property. Moreover, this solution also works for small areas, since there is no dividing element to break up the space. The platform is more like a vast, thick carpet that blankets the area and organizes the activities.

The modules ensure that each area has a sufficient amount of space for its needs.

The piece is more thn just a work surface for artists, as it can also function as a platform for displays and for providing service to the public.

The modules are independent and serve as individual workstations, but retain the same formal and functional language.

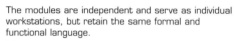

ARCHITECT: AIX ARCHITECTS
PHOTOGRAPHY: IGNACIO MARTÍNEZ
LOCATION: TISIS, AUSTRIA
DATE OF CONSTRUCTION: 2003
AREA: 860 SQ. FT.

Customs Office

The architects of this project wanted to design something that did not look like a typical border post. This striking structure includes a large roof, so thin it resembles paper floating in the air, that covers four rows of cars and, right in the middle, the customs office. This office, which was designed to be as space-efficient as possible, consists of a small glass box that provides a view of the activities taking place inside.

The light, slender, regular roof conceals its vast 9,000-square-foot metal framework. A great, projecting structure, the roof is supported by two columns of reinforced concrete that rest on a base almost as big as the roof itself. The small office is configured by a metal framework that sits on the same base.

The shape and proportion of this office are determined by its position. It is located on what was once the divider between rows of traffic, and consequently is long and narrow. On either end, heavy units were built as protection against possible accidents, and the sides are made of prefabricated panels. A solid socle edges and defines the space, while the rest is glass-enclosed for better integration with the exterior.

Instead of a solid building acting as a barrier, the
custom office's vast projecting roof defines the
border area.

Separating the box-shaped office from the projecting
roof emphasizes the structure's lightness. Artificial
illumination reinforces this effect at night.

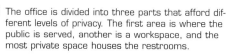

The office is divided into three parts that afford different levels of privacy. The first area is where the public is served, another is a workspace, and the most private space houses the restrooms.

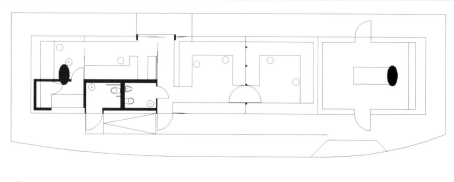

Plan

0   2   4

Rectangular birch plywood panels cover the interior.

ARCHITECT: ATELIER ARCHITECT ANDREAS SCHMITZER
PHOTOGRAPHY: CLEMENS LUTZ
LOCATION: SALZBURG, AUSTRIA
DATE OF CONSTRUCTION: 1998
AREA: 860 SQ. FT.

Raika Bank

The design of the Raika Bank in Salzburg represented an attempt to change the bank's classical image as an institution devoted exclusively to safeguarding money and securities. In the new design, information and transparency are essential values. Now clients can conduct their transactions themselves while the bank, providing an array of services, serves simply as support. In this respect, the imposing, monumental image of banking establishments, generally surrounded by security devices, has shifted to one of a small, welcoming, open space that invites a more intimate relationship between employees and clients.

The architectural design makes the leap from the traditional type of bank space to that of the new generation in the age of telebanking, the Internet, and virtual companies. This wide range of services called for a practical space that finds its expression in furnishings and workstations whose functions can change over time. Other transactions, such as loan applications, can be conducted in more private office spaces adjacent to the principal area. The corporate image is molded by materials, shapes, and colors that also convey a sense of functionality and high technology.

Some of the more private workspaces, such as conference rooms, are separated from the principal area by translucent floating panels.

The circular shape of the workstations emphasizes the notion of mobile furnishings that can be moved around within the space.

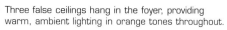
Three false ceilings hang in the foyer, providing
warm, ambient lighting in orange tones throughout.

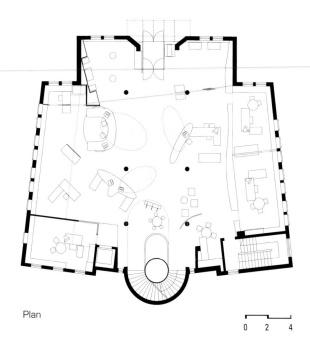

Plan

0   2   4

A curved wall integrates and separates all the
technical equipment as well as provides
storage space for the employees.

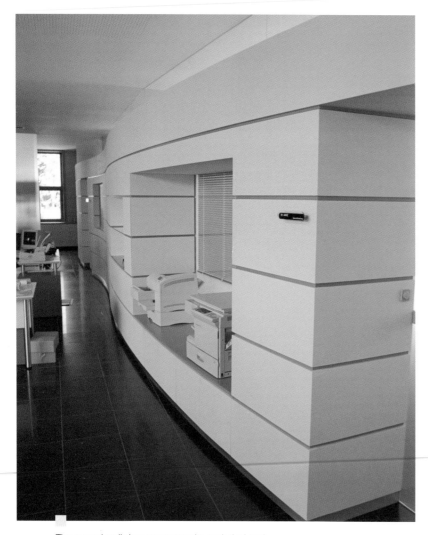

The curved wall that separates the technical and
service area from the rest of the space creates a
dynamic effect along the corridor.

The play of warm and cold colors reinforces the
formal character of the project.

ARCHITECT: SLADE ARCHITECTURE
PHOTOGRAPHY: JORDI MIRALLES
LOCATION: NEW YORK, NY, UNITED STATES
DATE OF CONSTRUCTION: 2000
AREA: 850 SQ. FT.

Geotext

Geotext, located in New York City, provides comprehensive language services ranging from the translation of short texts to 24-hour simultaneous interpretation. Its varied client base and the image of trustworthiness and reliability it wanted to project were pivotal to the design of this simple, functional space. Occupying a former industrial loft in the heart of the gentrified Chelsea district, the offices boast a set of large windows that look out on the city and flood the interior with light.

The point of departure for the design strategy was the company's need to maintain strict control over the documents being worked on at any given time. The shelving, which divides the work areas, also helps craft an image for the office. An internal system of metal supports makes it easy to change the height of each shelf to accommodate the size and number of documents on hand. Beiges and grays dominate the color scheme, accentuating the austere, neutral effect.

The reception area is dominated by a slender wooden
desk with an extension that swings upward.

The variety of subjects and projects the firm deals
with creates a need for flexible, independent
modules.

The entrance to the offices is marked by perforated plywood panels that create a texture recognizable from the foyer.

ARCHITECTS: TOM FAULDERS/BEIGE DESIGN,
KALLAN NISHIMOTO, YORAM WOLBERGER
PHOTOGRAPHY: BEIGE DESIGN, CÉSAR RUBIO
LOCATION: BRISBANE, CA, UNITED STATES
DATE OF CONSTRUCTION: 2000
AREA: 800 SQ. FT.

Cahoots

This client's business is to make the Internet more user-friendly through real-time voice exchanges. The company needed a space that would reflect their position as pioneers of creative and technological innovation. To this end, the architectural design strategy was based on establishing a work environment that marries the notions of space and image and the phenomena that go along with them, such as light transmission, pixelization, and acoustic vibration. The result is an architectural space that has the properties of digital space: it is changeable, interactive, and fluid.

The elevator leads to an entry hall, an orange tunnel in which the visitor is immediately stimulated by the sound of voices and footsteps. The two conference rooms adjacent to this access tunnel are constructed of perforated panels and colored lenses, reminiscent of digital screens with pixels, where each cell projects information independently in its unique position while together they form a single image. These architectural lenses literally change the perception of the spaces from the interior or exterior.

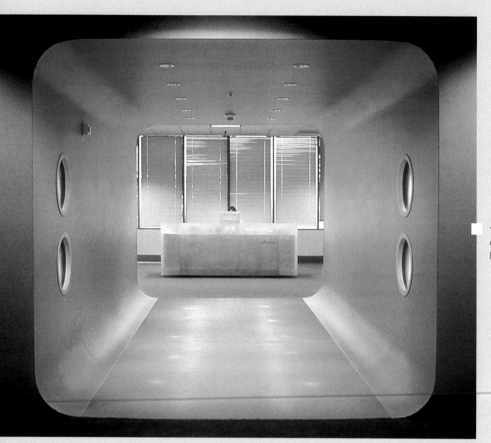

The access hall is a smooth, cornerless, seemingly endless space, and is the first altered space the public encounters.

A slender plastic divider shapes this conference room. The use of interior surface in architectural components is avoided as much as possible.

The design objective for the work area was to create individual spaces without compromising the sweeping interior views.

The work tables, translucent surfaces atop dots of color, are also based on optical properties.

ARCHITECT: SANT ARCHITECTS
PHOTOGRAPHY: JOHN EDWARD LINDEN
LOCATION: VENICE, CA, UNITED STATES
DATE OF CONSTRUCTION: 2000
AREA: 750 SQ. FT.

1613 Abbot Kinney

These offices are located on a popular commercial street in Venice, California. The client wanted space that could be used as a single unit or divided into two areas of 750 square feet each, to be rented separately. The special characteristics of the location, a low budget, and the client's requirements called for a clear, flexible design strategy. Therefore, the two office units were based on the same functional plan. When joined they work as a whole, but when they are separated each has its own identity.

Flexibility was achieved in harmony with the structural layout of this small building. The system is based on two sets of wooden beams that slope in opposite directions and cross at the center. The two sections of the butterfly roof meet at a large central truss that runs the entire length of the building and divides the two spaces. This truss both accommodates and makes it possible to remove the partition, a double panel of glass that lets light in while maintaining sound insulation.

A small loft has been fitted out at the end of the
building as an area where privacy is assured.

The façade and the modulation of the windows
reinforce the asymmetry of the two units, although
both enjoy access to the rear garden.

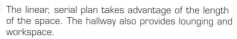

The linear, serial plan takes advantage of the length of the space. The hallway also provides lounging and workspace.

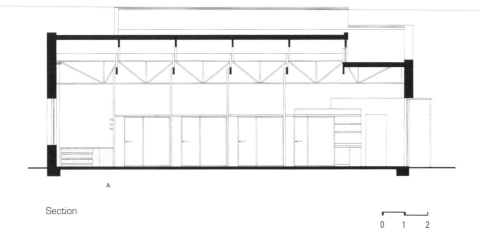

Section

0   1   2

Wood, the predominant structural material, is also present in the elements that shape and divide the interior space.

ARCHITECTS: JOSEP BAGÁ, MARTA ROVIRA
PHOTOGRAPHY: NURIA FUENTES
LOCATION: BARCELONA, SPAIN
DATE OF CONSTRUCTION: 1998
AREA: 540 SQ. FT.

Architecture Studio

This project transforms part of a typical Barcelona apartment into an architecture studio for two partners. Residential apartments in this part of the city are traditionally organized around a very long corridor that provides access to several rooms, which are for the most part poorly ventilated and illuminated. The existing partitions in this apartment were eliminated to create a loftlike space in which two open areas are connected by large sliding doors. This makes for better use of the space and improves the natural lighting and ventilation.

The designers imaginatively use work tools as decorative objects. Open shelves store reference books, files, and stationery. Placing the shelves along the perimeter makes the most of the available space and creates a cozy atmosphere. One of the two areas is used for group projects, with one table off to the side and another in the middle of the space, while the other area is more private and is used as a management office.

The glass table, in the middle of the workspace, is used for meetings, to assemble models, or to accommodate auxiliary staff.

The management office is also a reading room, which makes it more intimate and welcoming.

Worktables were placed by the windows to take advantage of the natural light.

The tables and built-in shelves use dark wood, keeping with the classic character of the original space.

ARCHITECT: XAVIER GOMÀ
PHOTOGRAPHY: NURIA FUENTES
LOCATION: BARCELONA, SPAIN
DATE OF CONSTRUCTION: 2000
AREA: 800 SQ. FT.

Xavier Gomà Studio

This office occupies the lower floor of a typical Barcelona villa, an old home surrounded by a garden. Once on the outskirts of the city, the neighborhood has been absorbed into Barcelona proper. While it was originally a vacation home, the building has been used for various purposes over the years. When he acquired the property in 1970, the architect had the idea of establishing his office there and placing his home above it, with a renovation that would retain the original character of the space.

A series of design strategies was employed to adapt the old structure for use as office space. The decision to turn the lower floor into offices precipitated many changes: restructuring many spaces, moving certain functions to the upper part of the house, and freeing up as much space as possible below to make it into suitable workspace. The original ceramic flooring, typical of these houses, was replaced by wood. That, along with paint and furnishings, gives the space a renewed, contemporary look.

Certain elements—such as the original stained-glass windows, which overlook the rear garden, and the molding—retain the character of the villa.

Direct access to the garden, which can be enjoyed most of the year due to the city's mild climate, gives the office a warm, homey feel.

A blending of furniture, artfully placed, makes the
most of the interior space.

The design of the structure, freestanding and
surrounded by garden on all sides, allows natural
light to pour into almost every nook and cranny.

ARCHITECT: PATRIZIA SBALCHIERO
PHOTOGRAPHY: ANDREA MARTIRADONNA
LOCATION: MILAN, ITALY
DATE OF CONSTRUCTION: 1998
AREA: 800 SQ. FT.

Designer's Office

Located in the old naval area of Milan, near the canals that crisscross the southern part of the city, this former carpenter's workshop was transformed by a young couple, both graphic designers, into their permanent office. The space is noteworthy for its high ceilings and the formal richness of the beams, metal sheeting, exposed brick, and large windows overlooking the rear garden. Many of the outstanding features were retained, to lend character and personality to the space, and new features were incorporated to convert it into a functional office and graphic design studio.

The workshop was divided into two units by a slender, airy, metal mezzanine that is situated in the rear and accommodates the office suite. Metal stairs lead to an entrance hall and a large work center that faces the rest of the unit, accentuating the feeling of spaciousness. Behind the work center are a smaller room, used as an office; the bathrooms; and another small office, which enjoys a view of the garden. The custom-designed contemporary furnishings are carefully juxtaposed with original elements to give the interior a flavor all its own.

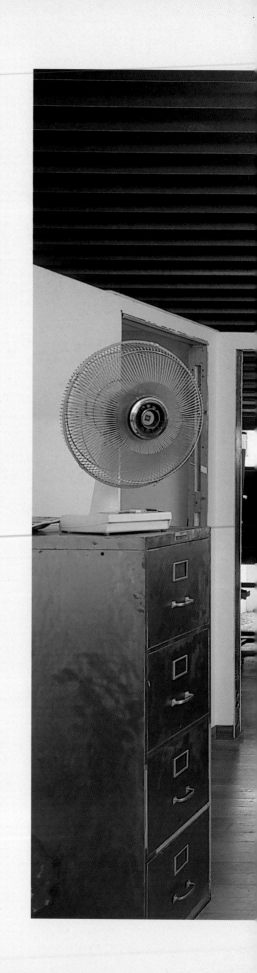

The mezzanine receives the benefit of the windows located on different levels.

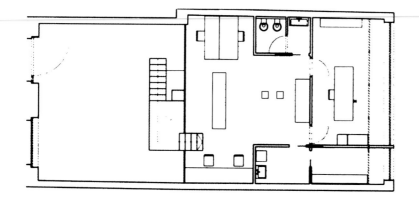

Plan

0 1 2

Part of the roof is made of translucent materials that let the natural light in. White awnings diffuse and filter it.

ARCHITECT: KENNEDY & VIOLICH ARCHITECTURE
PHOTOGRAPHY: BRUCE T. MARTIN,
KENNEDY VIOLICH ARCHITECTURE
LOCATION: BOSTON, MA, UNITED STATES
DATE OF CONSTRUCTION: 1999
AREA: 860 SQ. FT.

Printmakers Live/ Work Space

This space was designed for a prominent engraver who wanted to combine her engraving workshop, office, storage, and gallery in one place. The property had to be able to accommodate this plan and create an atmosphere related to her work. A former industrial space turned out to be ideal. The client's needs were analyzed to identify the spaces that required more privacy, those that had to be more public, and those that would need to integrate the two areas. What emerged was a workspace in which areas where the client can serve the public and areas where she can perform the more introspective work coexist in perfect balance.

The design includes a studio, a reception area, a gallery, an office, a library, and storage space. Each is an aesthetically pleasing juxtaposition of the artist's materials and finished work. The walls were finished with an iridescent plaster that changes color depending on the angle from which it is viewed. Glass panels separate some of the areas. They serve as reflecting screens at night, and during the day they allow natural light to flood the different areas.

The storage space was custom designed to
accommodate the work tools, canvases,
and finished works.

Even the work tools serve as decorative elements,
enriching the space with their textures, variety,
and colors.

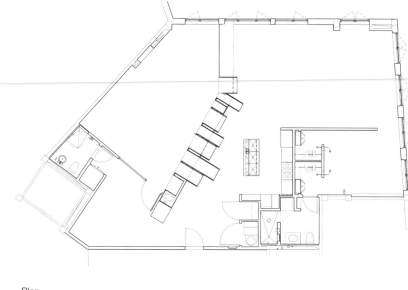

Plan

0   1   2

The glass partitions divide the different areas of the
loft while allowing natural light to enter every room.

ARCHITECT: BERND SPIEGEL
PHOTOGRAPHY: IGNACIO MARTÍNEZ
LOCATION: WOLFURT, AUSTRIA
DATE OF CONSTRUCTION: 1997
AREA: 698 SQ. FT.

Rohner Office

The Rohner office, the base of operations for a company that provides transportation and moving services, occupies a tiny plot next to the owners' home. This small annex is striking for its simple yet daring and functional appearance. It has all the advantages of being directly connected to the home, projects a strong image, and enjoys an ample terrace and a separate entrance. The requirements for this unit included having a corporate appearance and accommodating several workstations, a conference room, and a public service area.

The 20- by 30-foot rectangle sits slightly above the ground, and the street side is one and a half stories high. This touch allows for a greater presence in this semiurban setting, creating a new façade while still permitting a view of the façade of the home behind it. What's more, the glass creates a close relationship between the work areas and the exterior, making the interior space seem larger.

The structure consists of a system of wooden frames that make a flexible layout possible. While the exterior is finished in marble and metal, wood dominates the interior in the finishings, dividers, and furnishings.

Despite the narrow proportions of the reception area, located in the part of the unit with a two-story high ceiling, a sense of spaciousness is achieved thanks to its brightness and relationship with the exterior.